The Wisdom of John Pordage

Great Works of Christian Spirituality

New Grail

Library of Congress Cataloging-in-Publication Data
Pordage, John, 1607-1681.
 [Theologia mystica]
  The wisdom of John Pordage / [edited and introduced by Arthur Versluis].
  80 p. cm.-- (Great works of Christian spirituality ; v. 3)
  Drawn from the author's Theologia mystica (written with Edward Hooker)
  and his A treatise of eternal nature with her seven eternal forms.
  Includes bibliographical references and index. 6/04
  ISBN 0-9650488-7-X (alk. paper)
 1. Mysticism--Early works to 1800.I. Versluis, Arthur, 1959- II. Edward Hooker
 III. Pordage, John, 1607-1681. Treatise of eternal nature with her seven
 eternal forms. IV. Title: Treatise of eternal nature with her seven eternal forms.
 V. Title. VI. Series.

BV5082.3 P67 2003 .
248.2'2--dc21
                                            2002035802

©Arthur Versluis 2003

All rights reserved. No part of this publication may be reproduced, stored in a retrieval system, or transmitted in any form or by any means, electronic, mechanical, photocopying, recording or otherwise, without the prior permission of the publisher.

New Grail Publishing
St. Paul, Minnesota

www.grailbooks.org

New Grail Publishing
P. O. Box 14285
St. Paul, Minnesota 55114

The Wisdom of John Pordage

Contents

Introduction by Arthur Versluis . . . 1
Preface to the Reader by John Pordage . . . 27
What is God? . . . 28
The Eternal World . . . 32
Concerning Wisdom and the Most Holy Place . . . 47
The Seven Spirits and the Simplified Spirits of God . . . 49
On Eternal Nature . . . 55
The Abyssal Nothing and Eternal Nature . . . 59
On God in Eternal Nature . . . 77
The Archetypal Globe . . . 82
Index . . . 84

Volume III in *Great Works of Christian Spirituality*
Series Editor: Arthur Versluis

The Wisdom of John Pordage

Introduction by Arthur Versluis

This little book by John Pordage is the most lucid and comprehensive work on Christian mysticism I have ever read. It is remarkable, given the clarity and profundity of this work, that it has not been available or even noted by scholars since its original publication in 1683, two years after Pordage's death. But undeserved obscurity has been the fate of all Podage's works, the English originals of which have all been lost save what you hold in your hands, originally published under the title *Mystica Theologica*. Pordage's work is so extraordinary because it offers his direct spiritual experience in a rigorously organized, logical structure. If you think that the word "mysticism" means wooly-minded self-indulgence, prepare to be surprised. Here, Pordage offers nothing less than initiation into the deepest mysteries of Christian spirituality.

Who was John Pordage? The son of a London merchant, Pordage was born in 1607, and entered Pembroke College, Oxford, in 1623. It is possible that he obtained a diploma of a doctor of medicine at Oxford in 1640, but some scholars doubt this (Hutin 82). Certainly it is true in any case that he was not destined to practice medicine, but to be an exemplar of *homo religiosus*. For whatever his other schooling, Pordage entered into the order of the Anglican

Church and was made vicar of the church of St Lawrence's at Reading in 1644. Soon, under the auspices of Elias Ashmole, he was made rector of the rather wealthy parish at Bradfield, a position he held until 1654.

At Bradfield, Pordage's wife, Mary Freeman, an especially pious and spiritual woman whom he married for that reason, began to have visionary experiences. Soon Pordage himself was experiencing remarkable phenomena, including angelic apparitions, and these were witnessed too by others in a small group of theosophers who gathered around Pordage and his wife in a prayer group. This group was eventually to include men like Thomas Bromley and Edmund Brice—both of whom were educated at Oxford and themselves wrote theosophic treatises— and women like Anne Bathurst and Mrs Joanna Oxenbridge, both women of high society who left records of their spiritual journeys with the Pordages.

Pordage's visionary experiences began in August of 1649. This opening of the worlds was the revelation to Pordage and his family of the good and evil invisible realms that inform this visible world of ours. Pordage and his family saw firsthand the *Mundi Ideales*, or invisible realms, one full of love, the other of wrath. The wrathful realm was evidently quite unpleasant: Pordage and his family, he wrote, witnessed not only the presence of evil hierarchies— in monstrous theriomorphic forms, all "misshapen," with cat's ears and cloven feet and fiery eyes—but their physical manifestations in sulphuric foul odors and even the imprint of their images on the windows, ceiling, and chimney of the house. He and his wife, being unable to remove these various images from the chimney using wet cloths, resorted to smashing them off with hammers.

But Pordage wrote that he also passed through the flames and entered into paradise, which he called *Mundus Luminosus*, or the light world. Here there were "multitudes almost innumerable, of pure Angelical spirits, in figurative bodies as clear as the morning-star and transparent as crystal." Here they saw the rare beauty of these beings, felt the inexpressible joys and harmonies of heaven, smelled delightful heavenly scents, and heard celestial music. The "tongue can hardly express these odors of paradise," these glorious visions and sounds, Pordage wrote.

About this time, Pordage was tried before the local Anglican commission as an heretical minister of the faith. Against him were arrayed a whole range of charges, including provocative statements, and immoral conduct. Pordage was able to defend himself well against all these charges: the supposedly provocative or heretical statements imputed to him he proved to have been taken out of context and misinterpreted; the charge that he had kept a mistress in London he demonstrated to be quite false. Thus he was able to exonerate himself from the accusations, and he was allowed to continue as a minister from 1649 to 1654.

In the same period, Pordage's small group grew to include such remarkable people as Thomas Bromley and Edmund Brice. But in 1654, Pordage was tried again on the same charges, and despite his eloquent rebuttal, he was in fact removed from his ministerial position at Bradfield. One of the chief accusations against Pordage was "that he hath very frequent and familiar converse with Angels," and that when he was attacked by a dragon in his home, "his Angel stood by him and upheld him." Further, "That Mrs. Pordage and Mrs. Flavel had their Angels standing by them also, Mrs. Pordage singing sweetly, keeping time on her breast, and that his children saw the spirits coming into the house, and said, look there, Father. . . And the whole roof of the house was full of Spirits" (*Innocencie*, 14-15).

Some sense of the atmosphere in which Pordage's second trial took place can be gathered from his account of the judge's rancor. The judge evidently was prejudiced against Pordage from the beginning, growling to Pordage that he was worse than a felon, for all he knew, and that he had no objection to trying Pordage again on the same charges on which he had earlier been acquitted. Pordage did have legitimate reason to be upset, for even the very act under which Pordage was being tried was itself not instituted until a full year *after* those things with which he was charged had been reputed to take place!

In such an atmosphere, one is hardly surprised to find Pordage ousted from his pastorate, but his peroration is moving. He writes:

And now ye Ministers of *Berks*, my persecutors, tell me, what wrong or injury have I done you; have I lusted to preach in any of your Pulpits? Have I privately gone from parish to parish, or from house to house to get followers, or make proselites of your hearers? Have I publicly or privately railed against you or your Doctrines? Have I not lived privately in my own place, onely holding forth that strict, dying, resigning life, as the way to life eternal[?] Why then am I persecuted with so much fury, and violence, as though I were not worthy to live amongst you? The Lord judge betwixt you and me, and give you to consider and repent of what you have done (*Innocencie*, 79)

But although he was deprived of his livelihood, and although Pordage found himself in extremely difficult circumstances for the remainder of his life, these outward difficulties only served to intensify his, and his group's, convictions and inward life. Of course, their persecution did mean that for some years they lived spiritually in the "outer darkness" surrounded by wrath, suffering something akin to what St. John of the Cross called the "dark night of the soul." But eventually they were restored to angelic communications and to the spiritual light. Yet until his death, Pordage and his small group kept themselves out of public view and therefore censure.

Even when the Restoration took place under Charles II in 1660, and suspended clergymen were allowed to return to their positions, Pordage did not take this step, but remained quietly with his group of fellow theosophers. As a leader of a small, private, non-Anglican religious group, however, Pordage was constrained to meet with them and to live discreetly, for by 1664 such non-conformist meetings were again outlawed, and their leaders potentially at least subjected to fines and imprisonment. Worse, 1665 and 1666 saw the advent of the Great Plague and the great London fire, seen by many as signs of the

Apocalypse (fears intensified by the associations of the number 1666 with the number of the Beast in Revelation). Many people fled London, and Pordage and his group had to return to Bradfield to live, only returning to London in 1668, the year Mrs. Pordage died.

This time of outer difficulty also saw the most important affiliation of Pordage's life, in some respects: that between Pordage and Mrs. Jane Leade, who first felt called to join his group in 1663. She remained a member of his group, and in fact assumed leadership, especially after April, 1670, when, after her husband's death, she experienced a vision of the Holy Virgin Sophia, who called her to a virginal life (*Fountain* I.17). From this point on, she was to write a large number of extraordinary visionary treatises, and to become a central theosophical figure of her era. In 1674, she moved into Pordage's own house, at his request, so that together they could form a more powerful spiritual union.

During this time—from the early 1670's until his death in 1681— Pordage wrote most of his elaborate, lucid, and concisely expressed metaphysical treatises that belong to the tradition of the German theosopher Jacob Böhme (1575-1624). But Pordage only occasionally refers to Böhme directly, for all these treatises were based wholly and directly on his own spiritual experience, exemplary of which is the treatise *Sophia*, which consists in twenty-two daily journal entries dated from 21 June to 10 July, and which contains biographical data from the year 1675. Pordage's magnum opus, *Göttliche und Wahre*

Metaphysica, [*Holy and True Metaphysics*] was also written during this time, probably concluded in the year of his death, 1681.

But none of these works were published during his lifetime and, even more surprisingly, only two were published in English after his death. Although all his works had a wide private circulation, and were extremely influential in both England and the Continent, it remains a strange fact that Pordage's primary works—albeit written in English—were published only in German, and have been accessible only in that language to the present day.

The Wisdom of John Pordage consists in a modern version of the two works published in English: *A Treatise of Eternal Nature with Her Seven Essential Forms* (1681) and *Theologia Mystica, or the Mystic Divinitie of the Aeternal Invisibles, viz, the Archetypous Globe* (1683). *The Treatise of Eternal Nature* offers a general introduction to the concept of Eternal Nature, the "first original and true ground of all created beings and so of all true knowledge (*Eternal Nature*, preface)." Outward, physical nature, then, has its origin in an archetypal, pure realm of "Eternal Nature" similar to the Platonic realm of Ideas or Forms. Thus Divine Nature is "hid in Nature, as a Jewel in a Cabinet;" it is manifested in the Seven Essential Forms, and has its origin in the Abyssal Nothing, which is the "ground of all Essences, and yet no Essence to be seen in it," the "fruitful Mother of all Things." In Pordage's treatise, then, we see a visionary hierarchy or ascent from the natural world to the archetypal, to the Seven Essential Forms (the qualities informing existence), to the abyssal Nothing of God Himself.

While at first it appears that the entirety of *Theologia Mystica, or, The Mystic Divinitie* (1683) was written by John Pordage, in fact the first third of the book was written by his contemporary, Edward Hooker, and is far more chaotic and unclear than Pordage's measured final two-thirds of the book. Still, in the midst of Hooker's contribution to the volume, one finds the following initiatory levels or degrees: the first "way is by *Vision*, when the Spirit of God presents the heavenly species or Ideas to the internal senses of the inward man (65)." The second way is "Illumination," when the mind is "enlightened by a ray, or beam proceeding from the Holy Spirit." The third way is "Transportation or Translation," when the mind is caught up to paradise (66); and the fourth is the "Catachresis" or coming down of the Holy Spirit to the "essence of the soul, there to complete, finish, and accomplish the work of *Regeneration* and to fix it in its state of glorification," unveiling the New Jerusalem (69).

Thus we can see that Hooker outlines a deepening reciprocal relationship between the individual and spiritual illumination. The first step is the awakening of spiritual vision, and the ability to see the archetypal Ideas about which Pordage remarks, "those images and figures which the opening of the eye manifests are not shadows and empty representatives but real and substantial ones," "living and spiritful."(34, 37). After this opening of the inner eye, one's mind is illuminated by the Holy Spirit, and then is transported out of the body into paradise, after which comes the *Catachresis*, or the completion of regeneration, the glorification of the initiate. Thus we see a kind of reciprocal movement after the initiate's inner vision is opened, first the awakening of inner sight, then illumination, then visionary transport, then the return to earth and glorification of the initiate, or the uniting of the transcendent and the earthly, symbolized by the New Jerusalem.

One finds a similar pattern appearing in Pordage's own writing on the "Abyssal Globe." Pordage's work is about the awakening of the inner eye of the heart, which begins with the contemplative's recognition of the abyssal globe's existence, the globe representing the Mystery of God before being (25). Then the initiate's inner eye begins to open, and he sees the "ravishing and amazing sight" as he beholds "things themselves intellectually, which causes most inexpressible joys and ecstasies in the spirit of the soul, to which nothing in this world can be compared (34)." In the globe, there are three courts: Outward, Inward, and Inmost (16). The opening of the abyssal eye in the globe belongs to the Inward Court, and when this eye opens, its mysteries are also threefold: to wit, the mysteries of the Eye, of the Heart, and of the outflowing Breath (31-32).

What Pordage writes is not in conflict with the four degrees of initiation discussed by Hooker, but rather is a typically lucid and detailed explication of the actual stages of inner awakening and illumination. Pordage outlines what happens when the initiate first realizes the existence of the globe, what it means when the inner eye opens, the ravishing delights of the visionary faculty, then the opening of the eye in the heart that in turn allows insight into the nature of Deity itself, and finally into the mysteries of the breath (21, 26, 28). It is quite clear from what Pordage writes that he has himself passed through the series of stages he is outlining; as is usual in the whole of his work, it is more or less as though he is providing his reader with a road map. One is not too surprised, then, to learn that J.L. [Jane Leade, the leader of Pordage's circle after his death] writes in the same book of how Pordage's "outward body lay in passive stillness in this visible orb" for "the space of three weeks together (7)."

In *Theologia Mystica*, we travel with Pordage on his visionary journey, a journey the nature of which is clarified by the preface Jane Leade contributed. Leade writes:

> since my acquaintance with him *until the Time of his Death*, he was ever more employed in a internal contemplative Life: the Spirit in him still searching for the deep and hidden Mysteries of the Kingdom. And truly he was not only a *Seeker*, but a successful *Finder* of that rich Pearl of the Gospel (*Theologia Mystica* 2).

Pordage employs the images of the globe, the eye, the heart, and the breath to explain visionary spirituality, and the supreme illumination:

> The sight of the holy Trinity from the opening of the eye, in the inward court of the Holy Place, is a lively, operative, reviving, and yet amazing and surprising sight. . . . .No pen can

decipher it; it is only the spirit of the eye that can open itself (31).

This illumination is essentially a vision of the archetypes of all things:

This sight of God's attributes from the opening of the eye in the abyssal globe is both a ravishing and amazing sight, for you do not behold ideas or similitudes of things, but the things themselves intellectually, which causes most inexpressible joys and ecstasies in the spirit of the soul, to which nothing in this world can be compared (34).

This illumination is, even further, beholding God "face to face," in the Eye, the center of the Heart.

Pordage then writes of the Virgin Sophia, who is "co-essential" and""co-eternal" with the Holy Trinity, but not "co-equal" with them, for she is but a passive efflux of the Trinity, its glory and mirror. Finally, Pordage writes of the nature of the angelic spirits, their nature and qualities. The spirits possess a materiality and senses of their own: "These *Spirits* are endued with a spiritual kind of materiality from the Love-Essence in the Heart of God." Hence they are "endued with the spiritual senses of seeing, hearing, smelling, tasting and feeling, whereby they are inabled to discern the object of the still eternity." The spirits have their own language; they have one ear, one eye, one breath (details that underscore their unity) and their "food and drink" is power from the Trinity (87, 92). Pordage's treatise therefore leads us from the initial vision and cosmology, through the transmuting power of Sophia, into the angelic heavenly realm itself.

God, Pordage begins, is the Spirit of Eternity unknowable intellectually by anyone, complete unity and simplicity *knowable only to himself.* This self-knowing is central, because it is also why existence and beings came into being: they are the divine means of self-knowing through manifestation. This is the fundamental nature of all existence, which is called to know itself, to know its own nature as divine manifestation. Being comes to know itself through contemplative human experience.

Although we cannot know God in himself, since only he can know himself, we can know God in what Pordage calls the "globe of eternity." The globe of eternity is the sphere in which the Spirit of Eternity, the eternal divine unity and essence of essences, subsists. The globe of eternity is the sphere in which God may be known as "the highest purity, clarity and brightness of glory beyond all imagination," "free from all impurity and imperfection" (13). The globe of eternity is prior to the Fall; it is the realm in which the divine spirits exist prior also to the angels, and in it is no sin or imperfection; it is pure love. In the center of the globe is an eye, which is the eye of the Spirit that "looking into itself, and finding nothing besides itself, by dilating itself, gives a beginning and end to itself. . . .so that the globe of eternity is nothing else, but the dilation of the eye of eternity from the center to the circumference" (17). The globe of eternity is the realm in which God manifests *"himself to himself*: for the eye turning it self inward into itself, comes to know itself."

Entering into the globe of eternity, one sees the eye in three successive stages: in what Pordage calls the "outward court," the eye is closed or contracted; in the inner court, the eye is "dilated," and "in the Holiest of all the state and majesty of the Trinity is displayed" (23). By writing that the eye is closed, Pordage means that it is beyond expression, hidden in its own mystery, and as Böhme put it, about "the eye of the abyss," "we have no "pen, tongue, nor utterance to write or speak of it, only the eye of eternity leads the eye of the soul into it." In other words, the eye cannot be known except by knowing itself. This self-knowledge of the Divine is the inner court, the dilation of the eye into the globe. And the third stage is that in which "the eye discovers the mystery of itself, that is, by opening itself, it discovers and reveals what it is in itself."

This revelation of the eye to itself can be understood by the figure of an eye in a heart, around which is radiating divine breath or power, all of which is enclosed in a circle or sphere. The eye generates the heart, or to put it in Christian terms, the Father generates the Son, and from both of them irradiate the power of the Holy Spirit, all of them enclosed within the globe of eternity. Words or images do not reveal the Divine attributes to us, but rather the attributes "themselves only are the manifesters and revealers of themselves; and the Spirit of God alone has the key to unlock the eye, at the opening of which they [the divine attributes] are clearly and lively manifested.

So this writing can do no more than point you to the place where they may be intellectually seen" (35).

The Heart of God, Pordage continues, is "generated by himself, out of himself, and for himself." It is "of a flowing nature, like the sea, without bottom or bounds;" "it is in a perpetual motion, and in this motion there is a perpetual communication of itself, from itself, through itself, to itself; and this out-flowing of the Heart, is nothing else but the original Divine Purity, Righteousness, and Holiness" (41). The overflowing "sea of the Deity" fills the entire Abyss, and is such a rejoicing, triumphing, and amazing sight, that words nor ideas nor likenesses cannot fully represent it. But when "your spirits are let in," "O ye seekers of the Divine Mysteries," "then you will understand what this pen hath written."

Within the "still eternity," there are innumerable "simplified spirits," "appearing all like bright points, sparks, or eyes." These pure spirits, which are like stars, are "Lights from Light," and "nothing else but the eye of eternity multiplying itself through the unmeasurable extent of the still eternity" (77). These "simplified spirits" were brought forth directly out of the Deity in order to reflect and manifest it, "for had the Divine Nature always continued shut up in itself, in the still Eternity, without bringing forth itself," "it would never have been known to any," and so the divine "Goodness, Perfection, and Happiness" could be known by countless pure Eyes that "dwell upon the blissful contemplation of the triune Deity." They are "all equal in dignity and glory," alike "sharers in the powers, raptures and joys of the most holy place," all "members of the same body, viz., the Divine Love-Essence" (89). These spirits are prior to the Angels, who belong to a later stage of manifestation, that called "eternal nature."

"Eternal nature" comes forth out of the Divine Abyss, which relative to our spirits, is "empty, immense space" in which there is "nothing to be seen, no darkness, no fire, no light, no creature," but an "unsearchable deep without any Essence, though indeed it be the ground of all Essence, and that from whence Eternal nature's Essence proceeds" (112). "Eternal nature" is composed of Fire, Light, and the four eternal elements of Fire, Water, Air, and Earth. But the word "eternal," Pordage notes, is only to be applied in a provisional way to these "eternal elements," because in reality nothing is eternal except the absolute transcendence of the Divine Abyss itself. Still, one may use the term "Eternal" to describe these principles of original existence prior to temporal nature because by comparison to fallen temporal nature, they seem eternal (118).

Eternal Nature, as originally brought forth, is "a blessed and happy essence," "perfection,""all beautiful, all spotless, all happy; no strife, misery, or death to be found in any borders of her dominion" (148). It contains forms of darkness, bitterness, and anguish, it contains fierce fire and water, light, and air, but it also contains the crowning "love-fire-essence" wherein one mets with "eternal rest, liberty, and triumphant Joy, as being come to that point where the end has found the beginning and where the beginning and the end are joined together, never to be parted again forever." In other words, eternal nature is, to the seeking spirit, like a royal palace with a series of rooms through which one must pass before one enters the royal chamber of the divine presence. Eternal nature is the "silver-pipe" through which flows the golden oil of the union of love-fire-light, so that we may come to enjoy the "wonders of eternity" for ourselves. When we enter into the paradisal realm, Pordage explains, we are entering into the realm of Eternal Nature through which we must pass in order to realize our true nature, which is like a Pearl or Jewel hidden deep in a field. What is this field where this Pearl is hidden? It is, Pordage tells us, ourselves.

It is perhaps not surprising that Pordage remains the most profound and yet the least-known contemplative author of the past several centuries. His work is itself like a jewel hid in a field, and is so profound that he himself placed a warning at the head of *Theologia Mystica*. In his *caveat* to the reader, he suggested that we not judge prematurely what he has written, but instead read it carefully and contemplate it for ourselves and over time see what in it meets with our own subsequent contemplative experience. When we are considering such an exalted subject as the contemplative life, his advice to be cautious in our judgement is particularly wise. But of all the contemplative authors I have read, he remains the most valuable and the clearest.

The Wisdom of John Pordage is at heart about the mystery of our spiritual initiation and transfiguration.

In the New Testament, this mystery is revealed by Jesus only to three of his closest disciples: Peter, James, and John. In Matthew 17:1-13, we find the following: Jesus took these three disciples aside, to a high mountain, and there he was transfigured before them, so that his face shone like the sun, and his garments were white as light. They saw him speak with Moses and Elijah, and then a bright cloud overtook them. Out of the cloud came a voice that said "This is my beloved Son, with whom I am well pleased. Listen to him." When the three disciples came down from the mountain with Jesus, he instructed them not to speak of this vision to anyone "until the Son of man is raised from the dead." The disciples then asked him why the Scribes say that first Elijah must come, and he replied that Elijah had already come, and "is to restore all things," yet "they did not know him, but did to him whatever they pleased. So also the Son of man will suffer at their hands."

The transfiguration revealed only to three disciples on a mountain is surely one of the most esoteric points in the four gospels. Jesus chose only a few disciples to whom he revealed this mystery, and even those three he commanded to remain silent about it during his lifetime. Further, when Jesus spoke of it afterward, he referred to Elijah, who is to "restore all things." Here we see the linked themes of transfiguration and what is often called "apocatastasis," or the restoration of all things. Christ transfigured is intimately interwoven with universal restoration that, like a jewel hid in a field, lies at the heart of a disfigured world in which even the Son of man must suffer. In other words, at the very heart of a suffering world is its own transfiguration, even if we see it not.

The contemplative path leads toward this transfiguration and universal restoration; it leads toward the salvation of the world. The contemplative path is not so much, as it is sometimes portrayed, an effort to escape from suffering, but rather brings about the transfiguration of the world by that which is beyond suffering. It is true that not everyone is ready for a contemplative journey, any more than all the disciples were ready for the vision of transfiguration. But those who are ready are so *in loco omnia*, or in the place of all. It was the poet Novalis who wrote that man is meant to be the "messiah of Nature," and this expresses something of what we see hinted at in the New Testament transfiguration: a few are chosen to be the vehicle of transfiguration, called to the contemplative path that leads into the most profound mysteries of all.

Conclusions

I have offered here a fairly thorough discussion of the English theosophic initiatory process as it is found in the work of Pordage, and now would like to step back from the details of this process and consider its implications and significance. The first implication concerns the transcendence of time and space. In modernity, we are conditioned to think exclusively in temporo-spatial terms, usually in terms of "progress" or "evolution" though time. This perspective derives in large part from the conventional Augustinian Christian view of history as extending from Christ's birth through the second coming, or in Teilhardian terms, from "Alpha" to the "Omega point." The scientific evolutionary theories of the twentieth century, as the example of Teilhard de Chardin demonstrates, had much in common with the historical emphasis of conventional Christianity both Protestant and Catholic. The theosophic initiatory process of John Pordage, in contrast, offers a totally different form of Christianity.

In the theosophic initiatory process as outlined by Pordage, the individual progressively realizes freedom from temporo-spatiality. The individual realizes his or her potential not in history, but in the transcendence of history. History is really the chronicle of those under the domination of the *spiritus mundi*, of fallen humanity under the influence of greed, lust, power-hunger, egotism, various forms of misery-producing ignorance. The theosophic initiate follows a path beyond the *spiritus mundi*, beyond the tragic history of fallen humanity, progressively transcending selfishness and entering into illumination that is indivisible from light, life, and love. Such a course does not entail abandoning one's humanity, but rather in fully realizing it as it is meant to be, free from suffering and full of joy.

This said, it is also true that such a path does not entail a selfish ignoring of those still caught in the suffering of history. Rather, one who has realized the upper stages of this initiatic process then has much deeper insight into what motivates people who have not undertaken initiatic inner work, and humbly seeks to guide them out of their fallen and tragic condition. This is the high degree of spiritual realization that Hooker refers to as *catachresis*, a Greek word deriving from the roots *kata* [completely] and *khristhai* [to use], meaning "to use fully" or "to realize potential completely." *Catachresis* refers to the complete accomplishment and "fixing" of the state of glorification, associated also with the image of the New Jerusalem, which is not in this context an imagined utopia at the end of history, but rather the image of heaven and earth united in the glorified initiate. This accomplishment does take place on earth and among others; it represents the union of the divine and the human that is precisely the meaning of Christ's life on earth. The initiate realizes Christ, and like Christ, seeks to bear the burdens of others and to assist others to realize this same joyous union of divine and human, the culmination of what it means to be alive.

When we look at Pordage's and Bromley's works, as indeed at the whole of English theosophic literature, it becomes quite clear that these authors are referring to a single theosophic initiatic process that entails the opening of inner vision and access to what Pordage calls in *Sophia* a "magical earth," what Bromley describes as when "our internal eye is more unlocked, to behold the paradisical world, with those luminous objects and inhabitants that are in it." The "magical earth" seen in spiritual vision is precisely what Henry Corbin called a *mundus imaginalis*, or imaginal realm: it represents an intermediate state between the duality of earthly life and the inexpressible unitive realization of total transcendence.

This visionary realm belongs neither to the realm of the subjective (fantasy) nor to the objective (scientific observer), but rather represents a realm in which subject and object reflect one another and ultimately are indivisible from one another. In Pordage's account, for instance, the initiate (the subject) perceives the divine object (if we may so put it) as joyous presence—as delight-filled taste, touch, smell, and so forth. Boundaries between self and other are dissolving, not only here, in the visionary realm, but also in the theosophic initiatic circle as well. Each individual is able to perceive the joys and sorrows of the others even at a distance because habitual divisions into self and other are being transcended.

Thus it would be totally mistaken to attempt to place a great divide between Pordage's visionary gnosis and the *via negativa*. I have elsewhere argued that *via positiva* gnosis both leads into and manifests *via negativa* gnosis; that spiritual symbolism both reveals and reflects sheer transcendence.[15] Here we have a case in point. Pordage in particular explicitly recognized the crucial importance of the Böhmean *ungrund*, or not-ground, the sheer transcendence that is the godhead, prior to all being. This is the "abyss" of the "abyssal globe" that Pordage's inner eye perceives at the opening of its visionary experience; it is the essential nature of paradise itself. Pordage's spiritual vision here is very much akin to what we find in Vajrayana Buddhism, particularly in the Nyingma tradition, where it is not at all uncommon for someone who is spiritually realized to have visionary experiences as part of their initiatic path. These visionary experiences are not seen in the tradition as somehow opposed to or fundamentally different from the fundamental nature of existence as *sunyata*, or emptiness, but rather as visionary revelations *of* that fundamental nature expressing itself in revelatory form.

It is important to observe that the word "initiation" has the meaning of "to begin," and this is very much implied throughout these accounts of theosophic initiation. Initiation in a theosophic context is most definitely a continuing process, and even what we see here as an end—*catachresis*—is only the beginning of another stage, the living out of the Christic life. For Pordage, this life was lived largely in reclusion, rather in the manner of a Sufi *shaikh* and disciples. Indeed, much of the theosophic initiatic tradition reminds us of Sufism, not least the visionary recitals of Pordage's major works, *Göttliche und Wahre Metaphysica*, *Vier Tractätlein*, and *Sophia*. Pordage left behind a vast *corpus* of works that, taken as a whole, very much suggest he was like an explorer who had entered into a new terrain and had set out to map it for all who would follow after him into it.

Taken as a whole and in the context of such works as Henry Corbin's *Spiritual Body, Celestial Earth*, the writings of Pordage, and his fellow theosophers do indeed suggest that there is a *terra lucida* to which we may have access through spiritual vision. While scientists sought to explore and manipulate the outer world during the eighteenth through the twentieth centuries, Western society was entirely neglecting the inner realms; it abdicated our spiritual calling in favor of *tekhné*, our increasing ability to control the physical realm. All the while, there remains an entire inner terrain that calls out for exploration, and whose exploration is synonymous with inner fulfillment. Yet we must keep in mind that this inner exploration can only take place at a price—that of our own ignorance, oftentimes the most painful of prices. This journey is not merely that of a "neutral" and manipulative observer, but rather the transmutation of the observer into that which is observed. To enter the *terra lucida*, we must give up our ordinary habitual selves and be willing to undertake the most fundamental adventure of all, that of our own transfiguration.

For it is self-evident that the initiatic journey Pordage outlines is nothing less than a radical, total transformation of the individual. It is not that the visionary realms which the soul traverses are its own creation—that would be mere solipsism—but rather that the soul must leave behind everything it holds dear, indeed, everything, including its concepts of itself, in order to enter into a realm where it gradually realizes its own joyous unity with all that transcends it. Held onto as a visionary event by a discrete self, even visionary experience can become an impediment. In its very nature, then, this is a path that is closed to all who refuse the radical openness it requires as a *sine qua non*. No wonder that it has remained so little known in the Christian world! Indeed, what you are now reading is the only specific discussion of this Christian initiatic path in print.

Having looked closely at Pordage's work, these words of the historian of religions Mircea Eliade take on renewed significance:

> It must never be forgotten that initiatory death simultaneously signifies the end of the "natural," noncultural man, and passage to a new modality of existence—that of a being "born to spirit," that is, a being that does not live solely in an immediate reality. Thus initiatory death forms an integral part of the mystical process by which the novice becomes another. . . .This is as much as to say that one becomes truly a man in proportion as one ceases to be a natural man and resembles a Supernatural Being (132).

These remarks of Eliade correspond to what we find in the writings of Pordage, and those of the other English theosophers. Theirs are truly accounts of initiatory death and rebirth, of being born into a new "modality of existence," of ceasing to be a natural man and becoming instead a transfigured and illuminated one whose goal then becomes to assist others toward realizing transcendence too.

Select Bibliography

The Wisdom of Pordage is drawn from:
John Pordage and Edward Hooker, *Theologia Mystica, or the Mystic Divinitie of the Aeternal Invisibles, viz, the Archetypous Globe*, (London: 1683)
John Pordage, *A Treatise of Eternal Nature with Her Seven Eternal Forms*, (London: 1681)

Selected Other Works by Pordage:
Pordage, John, *Innocencie appearing through the dark mists of pretended guilt*, (London: 1655)
____, *Göttliche und wahre metaphysica*, (Frankfurt: 1715)
____, *Ein gründlich philosophisch Sendschreiben*, (Amsterdam: 1698)
____, *Sophia: Das ist die holdseelige ewige Jungfrau der Göttlichen Weissheit*, (London: ca. 1675; Amsterdam, 1699)
____, *Vier Tractätlein*, (Amsterdam: 1704)

Secondary Works

Henry Corbin, *Spiritual Body and Celestial Earth, From Mazdaean Iran to Shi'ite Islam*, (Princeton: Princeton UP, 1977)

Mircea Eliade, *Rites and Symbols of Initiation* (New York: Harper, 1958)

Antoine Faivre, *Access to Western Esotericism*, (SUNY: 1994)

Serge Hutin, *Les Disciples anglais de Jacob Boehme aux XVIIe et XVIIIe siècles*. (Paris: Editions Denoël, 1960)

Nils Thune, *The Behmenists and the Philadelphians: A Contribution to the Study of English Mysticism in the 17th and 18th Centuries*. (Uppsala: Almquist and Wiksells, 1948)

Arthur Versluis, *Theosophia: Hidden Dimensions of Christianity*, (Hudson: Lindisfarne, 1994)

____, *Wisdom's Children: A Christian Esoteric Tradition*, (Albany: SUNY, 1999)

____, *Wisdom's Book: The Sophia Anthology*, (St. Paul: Paragon House, 2000)

The Wisdom of John Pordage

To the Reader:

Judicious reader,

So would I have you to be. Read, then weigh, and seriously consider what you read, and then reject what you don't like. But don't rashly condemn what in your present state you cannot comprehend. Let it lie, for it may be better understood in another state. The author's philosophy proceeds from the center, and not from others, so he writes in an unknown way and unusual method. At first, reading the style may seem something unpleasant, but let patience be your companion to carry you in reading it from beginning to end, and the bitterness may be turned into a sweet pleasantness, and cause a delight in your reading it over a second time. I only court your appetite to read it over with judgement, and then judge what you please. I write not to gain disciples, nor to make a sect or party, nor to make divisions in the world. There are too many sects, schisms, and divisions in the world already; but I wish only to declare the interest of truth, who is able to preserve herself from all the falsities of this present age. Therefore do not blind your own mind with prejudices before you read, for how then should you understand what you read? So I rest.
yours in the love of Jesus
John Pordage, M.D.

What is God?

What is God, that was before the globe of eternity was brought into manifestation?
I answer: By God in this place I understand the Spirit of Eternity himself, as he is an eternal unity and simplicity. But what this eternal unity and simplicity of himself is, who can tell but himself, it being unknowable to any besides himself? For no creature can comprehend an infinite, unsearchable, and incomprehensible Creator; therefore none can know what the Spirit of Eternity is but himself alone. The first manifestation of himself is in the globe of eternity, for there he first becomes knowable to intellectual creatures, but without and beyond it, he is as a Nothing to all created understandings, being hid and wrapt up in his own unsearchable Mystery.

The nature of the Holy Trinity as they exist in the globe of eternity, without and before eternal nature, is a very great mystery. Many disapprove that the word *Person* be applied to the Trinity, because their spirits, in the sight of vision and the light of revelation, never could perceive any personality in the Holy Trinity. And indeed nothing is more true than that there are no figurative persons in the Deity. Neither does the Scripture in any place tell us of three persons in the Trinity, but when it speaks of the Trinity, it expresses itself by referring to the three and the one. Hence it is that mystical writers, instead of the word *Person*, make use of number to signify the Trinity by calling the Father *Monas*, the Word *Duas*, and the Holy Ghost *Trias*. And if all would keep to these expressions, it would take away much contention about words.

What is God the Father?
Answer: God the Father is the first original beginning of the Trinity: were there no beginning, there could be no end; were there no first number, there could be no second or third in the Trinity.

What is God the Son?
God the Son is the second number of the Trinity. Were there no Son, there would be no Father. He is the center and heart of the Trinity. He is generated of the Father before the eternal world and eternal nature came into being.

What is the Holy Ghost?
He is the third and completing number of the Trinity. He is an outflowing breath, life, or power, which proceeds from the Father through the Son, and executes the will of the Father. This outflowing life and acting power proceeds from the Divine essence of the Father and the Son, and therefore is co-eternal, co-essential, and co-equal with the Father and Son.

What is the nature of the Holy Trinity?
I answer: it is pure unity, and pure unity is pure Deity; and this is the nature of the Father, Son, and Spirit. And as they have but one undivided nature, so

they have but one Eye, one understanding, one will. But if anyone inquire further what this eternal unity and Deity is, I answer that no one knows save the unsearchable Trinity. Neither is it any further knowable by angels or men but that it is what it is. Still, if the Unity is unknowable *in itself*, yet it may be known through the Trinity. For if the nature of the Trinity be eternal unity and simplicity, free from all contrariety and mixture, it follows that light and darkness, love and anger cannot be in the Holy Trinity, as they exist in the Globe of eternity.

Some may answer that God is styled in Scripture as angry, and in other places as light and love. But I reply that these Scriptures speak of God as he has introduced himself into impure nature's essence after the Fall, whereas I am speaking of God as he exists in eternal nature before it was divided by the fall. The Holy Trinity is nothing but eternal unity, free from any contrariety or mixture whatever.

The Holy Trinity are in themselves a free eternal liberty. They are free from all essences whatsoever and exist in their own eternal liberty.

The Holy Trinity's nature is all happiness and blessedness: no misery, torment, or anguish is to be found in them, or proceeds from them. Hell, death, and the curse never proceeded from the Holy Trinity, because their nature is all happiness.

The Holy Trinity are complete in themselves, as nothing can be added to them, or taken from them, rejoicing from Eternity to Eternity in their own fullness, completeness, and absolute perfection. The eternal world and eternal nature were not created out of necessity, as if the Holy Trinity had stood in need of them, for the Trinity was completely perfect and happy before these came into being, and would continue so if they were no more.

The Unity of the Divine Nature is nothing else but love. In the eternal world, in eternal nature, and in the angelical world, there is no other manifestation but that of love. For the Holy Trinity who manifest themselves in these worlds' principles are themselves nothing but love.

Love is the *Alpha* and *Omega*, the beginning and ending Essence of all essences. We cannot ascend higher than this love, because there is no essence above, before, or beyond it. As in number we cannot pass beyond a unity, first of numbers, and so neither can we, when we speak of essences, go beyond the love-essence, which is all and all in the eternal world, which is the first and beginning of all worlds.

Blessed, thrice blessed are those who have found love and enjoy it.

The Eternal World

I call the Eternal World the globe of eternity, for so it was when I was taken up to have a view of it. In the globe of eternity, I distinguished three distinct places, which yet make up but one undivided globe or sphere. The first of these places was the outward court, the second the inward court, and the third as the inward court or the holy place. My guide first led me into the outward court, where I took notice of two things: the globe, or circumference itself, and the second the eye placed in the center of the globe. This globe is not created by God, but generated out of himself, and is substantial, though a very refined and spiritual substance, for it is the essence of essences, and substance of substances.

The eye in the center of this globe represents the spirit of eternity, which is God himself, who manifests himself in the center of the globe as an eye. This essential eye of God, looking into itself, and finding nothing besides itself, by dilating itself forms the globe of eternity.

Why did God form this globe of eternity? First, that he might dwell therein as in an house or mansion. Second, for the manifestation of *himself to himself*, for the eye turning itself inward into itself, comes to know itself, and to see, feel, and taste itself, and if it look outward, it sees nothing but itself, because as the eye is God, so is the globe nothing but the dilation of the eye.

This globe is the cause and original ground from whence all other principles proceed. It is an all-comprehensive globe, because it contains all other globes and principles whatsoever, but it is itself comprehended by none. This globe is nothing other than the spirit of eternity's dilating itself, and so if there were anything out of the bounds of this globe, it must also be out of the comprehension of the spirit of eternity, which cannot be, because this spirit is God himself, who is all in all, and contains all worlds, centers, and creations.

But, you'll say, if the spirit of eternity be incomprehensible and infinite, how can it be contained and comprehended in the globe of eternity? To which I answer that such a being cannot be comprehended or contained by anything but itself; so when we say that God is incomprehensible, we do not mean he is not comprehended by himself, but only that nothing besides himself can comprehend him.

This is an abyssal globe, and an abyssal eye, of an unsearchable depth, without bottom or ground; but the abyssal eye, looking downwards into itself, and finding nothing but itself, did set a bound to itself. And thus this abyssal globe of eternity was formed in height, depth, and breadth, all this in the twink of an eye, for the eye looking up gave it height, looking down gave it depth, and on each side gave it breadth. This is the outward court of the glorious palace of the king of kings. Himself is the builder, himself the matter of it, and therefore the matter of this palace may well be called almighty matter, but not the matter of this outward world, as some would have it to be.

The eye in the globe is the seat of the spirit of eternity, God himself in his own pure simple abstracted essence, before introducing himself into the principle of eternal nature. The abyssal eye is the first being of all beings, none before it nor beyond it; for it is nothing but the first manifestation of the spirit of eternity. Nothing can be prior to it.

In the outward court, the eye of eternity is shut; in the holy place, the eye is dilated; and in the holiest of all, the state and majesty of the Trinity is displayed.

The contraction of the eye is God shutting himself up in his own mystery; here the eye of eternity only appears as the point and center of the globe of eternity. The whole fullness of the Deity is contained and as it were locked up in this contracted eye, which gives being to the outward court. This contracted eye or center represents the Deity as he hides himself in his own mystery, for he is the most absolute and first unity, invisible, indivisible, without organs, shape, or figure. What can be more proper to represent such a being than the point or center of a circumference, which in itself is invisible, and without parts, shape, or figure?

The highly illuminated Jacob Böhme gives us this following account concerning this contracted eye of the Deity: "It is the eye of the abyss, concerning which we have no pen, tongue, nor utterance to write or speak of it, only the eye of eternity leads the eye of the soul into it, and so we see it, else it must remain in silence and this hand could not describe anything of it."

As long as the eye is shut, the whole globe of eternity is the outward court, but as soon as the eye is opened, it is the inward court, for the Deity manifesting himself makes the outward court to disappear, and presents the inward. No spirit can pass at will from the outward corut to the inward, but must await the opening of the eye.

The first mystery discovered at the opening of the abyssal eye is the mystery of the being and existence of God in himself, before eternal nature or any creatures were.
Now as God by the opening of the eye discovers himself to be the spirit of eternity, existing in and filling the globe of eternity, so is the spirit of eternity manifested to be all-power, universal power and pure act, as the School-men term it, filling the whole and every part of the globe of eternity. This spirit of eternity is all power, one undivided power, a perfect unity without any separation, distinction, or division.

The spirit of eternity is not only essential and substantial in itself, but also the primary essence of all essences, and substance of all substances.
No power can be without essence, and no essence without power.

But, you'll say, if the spirit of eternity is the beginning of all things, and the essence of all essences, then does it follow that God is the beginning of evil essences as well as of good? To which I answer: when we say that the spirit of eternity is the essence of all essences, it must be restrained to good essences, actions, and motions, which proceed from the spirit of eternity, and not extended to those that are evil. For there is nothing but God himself manifested in the abyss of eternity, and no evil essence to be found in him, so it must follow that the eye of eternity manifests only God, for it is plain that no evil can be in God.

Yet how can this unity not be in conflict with the nature of the Trinity?
I answer: Though eternal unity cannot consist with an absolute division, such as between things that subsist independently of one another, yet things can be in one another, united in the root of unity.

For an illustration, look at the figure on the following page.

The round circle represents the abyssal globe, the eye in the midst of the heart, represents the Father, the generator of the Son, who is the heart of the Father. A

And the outflowing of power, like a breath, represents the Holy Ghost, proceeding from the Father through the heart of the Son. The Father is one with the Son, and the Spirit proceeds from the union of them both. Wherever the eye is, there is the heart, and there also the outgoing power streams forth from them. Yet the eye is not the heart, nor the outgoing breath either eye or heart.

  I know there are many who are so great enemies of the word *Person* that they suppose the Father, Son, and Spirit to be only three denominations, but this is a great mistake, for the eye of the Father is an essential power, not a mere denomination; the Son is an essential being, generated out of the Father, and the Holy Ghost is an essential breath proceeding from the Father's eye through the Son's heart.

When the eye is closed, then neither the eye of the Father, nor the Son's heart, nor the breathing forth of the Spirit is to be seen, but when the eye opens, then the heart of the Son and the Holy Ghost are seen, so when the Eye of Unity in the Center opens, then the blessed Trinity becomes visible. So we see that the Unity is in Trinity, and the Trinity in Unity.

The sight of the Holy Trinity, from the opening of the eye in the inward court of the holy place is a lively, operative, reviving, and yet amazing and surprising sight, a sight worth the whole world. No pen can decipher it on paper; it is only the spirit of the eye that can open itself and give you the living and ravishing sight of its own essentiality without similitudes or figures, though one can express it outwardly no better than I have in the foregoing figure.

Let no man object here that I do not make use of Scripture for the confirmation or illustration of these deep mysteries, for the Holy Scriptures speak of God as he has introduced himself into eternal nature, and not as he exists out of and before eternal nature, in the globe of eternity. Therefore you must not expect my alleging of Scriptures whilst I am treating a subject that they do not reveal. Still, it is certain that the opening of the Eye cannot discover anything contrary to Scriptural revelation, though it cannot be so readily confirmed from Scripture. If my subject were to speak of the Fall and the Redemption of sinners by Christ, I should not be wanting to confirm my writing from Scripture; but as long as I am writing of the solitary being of God in the globe of eternity, the spirit of God in the eye must be my guide and witness.

The third opening of the eye discovers the mystery of itself, that is, by opening itself, it discovers and reveals what it is in itself. To speak more particularly, this third opening of the eye manifests all those powers commonly called the attributes of God, for this eye of the abyss sparkles forth from itself its own perfection, beaming forth its own beauty in lustrous rays, like the sun. These beams proceeding from the eye are God's eternity, infinity, immensity, incomprehensibility, omnipotency, as the outflowing powers and perfections of the eye. They are God's essential perfections, without which he cannot be God. St. Paul says that this visible creation manifests God's eternal Godhead and power, and so it is, but if so, how much more does the abyssal globe, the first mansion of the Holy Trinity, manifest all the eternal attributes and powers of his Godhead?

This sight of God's attributes from the opening of the eye in the abyssal globe is both a ravishing and amazing sight, for you do not behold ideas or similitudes of things, but the things themselves intellectually, which causes most inexpressible joys, and ecstasies in the spirit fo the soul, to which nothing in the world can be compared. Nor can any letters, words, or images discover this attributes to us, but themselves only are the revealers of themselves, and the spirit of God alone has the key to unlock the eye, at the opening of which they are clearly and lively manifested. So this writing can do no more than point you to the place where they may be intellectually seen and discerned.

The fourth opening of the abyssal eye discovers and manifests the eternal faculties of the Godhead—his intellect, will, and divine senses, under which are comprehended his wisdom, prescience, and omniscience.

But you will say that these faculties, as likewise the senses of seeing, hearing, tasting, smelling, and feeling, are only attributed to God to comply with our weakness, and to make him intelligible to our understanding, not that there are any such faculties or senses in God, but only by way of analogy. To this I reply that the forementioned faculties and senses are most really and truly in God, even more really than they are or can be in any creature, for in him they are originally and in truth, and in the creature only by way of participation. Understanding, will, wisdom, hearing, see, and so forth are in God primarily, essentially, and in the creature only derivatively and by way of resemblance, as the copy resembles and expresses its original.

And you will further object that by attributing these faculties and senses to God we seem to espouse the error of the anthropomorphites, who supposed the spirit of eternity was in the likeness of a man. But the anthropomorphites framed God after the image of a man, whereas we attribute these faculties and senses to God after a divine manner, primarily, originally, as is consistent with the super-excellence of the divine being. Further, we say that these faculties and senses are in God after a spiritual manner, without being fixed to particular and distinct members or organs, which cannot be in God, as he is a spirit, and is a perfect unity in himself.

We now proceed to a further consideration of this eye. The abyssal eye is God's face, for when this eye fully opens upon us, then we see God face to face, that is, clearly as he is in his own essence, without any veil or covering. When this eye beams forth its brightness upon the spirit of the mind, then God's face is said to shine upon us, and the shutting of the eye is when God hides his face from us. This eye is the face of the total Trinity, not only that of the Father.

The fifth opening of the abyssal eye manifests and discovers the heart of the Deity. Here is discovered the relation of the heart to the eye. The heart is the seat and resting place of the eye, for the eye is in the center of the heart. They are co-equal and co-essential.

This heart is the very life itself of the Deity, for God has no soul, neither can he have any, for all souls proceed from the womb of eternal nature, but the spirit of eternity, of whom we here speak, is before eternal nature had any being. God has no soul because he has no need of one, his heart supplying the place of a soul, and in this he is distinguished from all angels and men, none of which are without souls.

The essential heart of God is generated by himself, out of himself, and for himself. The heart of God is of a flowing nature like that of the sea, without bottom or bounds; it is like a spring and bubbling well that can never be drawn dry; it is in perpetual motion, and in this motion there is perpetual communication of itself, from itself, through itself, to itself, and this outflowing of the heart is nothing but the original divine purity, righteousness, and holiness. The heart of God is the overflowing sea of the Deity which flows from himself, from his own original purity, into the wholly eternal abyss with its fullness. It is so immense in its flowing forth that the deep abyss of the eternal globe would not be able to contain it, except that the spirit of the eye in his omnipotency sets bounds to the outflowing of his own divine nature. And this outflowing ocean of the Deity is, by the opening of the eye, manifested to be a clear, transparent mist or vapor, filling the whole deep of the abyssal globe.

This sight from the opening of the abyssal eye is a lively, spiritful, rejoicing, triumphant, and amazing sight, and cannot be expressed in dead words or letters, neither can any idea, form, or likeness fully represent it, as it discovers itself by the opening of the eye. O ye seekers of the divine mysteries, when your spirits are let in to a sight of this divine mist, then you will understand what this pen has written.

The heart is the fixed center and fountain of the outgoing, overflowing ocean of the Deity. This heart is an ever-rising, bubbling spring of living waters, which fails not, for the fulness of the Deity is continually flowing, streaming forth from the heart, and returning to it again. The heart is the treasury of life in the Deity. It bears the image of the whole Deity.

The divine nature is nothing but love, seated in the essential heart of God, from which it streams forth and returns again. It is God's flaming heart, because the essential love continually burns and flames in it. This eternal love, the unchangeable nature of God, is a most pure virgin, love without lust or desire; it wills nothing but the will of God.

What pen can express the high purity of this eternal love? It is eternal liberty, being free from all things. It cannot mingle with anything of nature contrary to itself; it is free from all things, and all things are free from it.

But you will object that the Scriptures tell us that God has no image. To this I answer that God indeed has no organic outward image resembling those of angels and men. But Scripture does not contradict God's having an essential inward form or image, according to which image, we are told in Genesis 1, God created man.

The opening of the eye in the heart reveals God's divine qualities, virtues, and excellencies, which proceed from the heart of God. These include his love, purity, truth, faithfulness, unchangeableness, goodness, perfection, righteousness, and holiness.

I searched diligently, and found that no pardoning mercy, nor justice, nor wrath, nor death, curse, anguish, sorrow, darkness, evil, or elements were to be found in the solitary abstractness of the Deity. I say no pardoning mercy because there was nothing besides himself, and so no object that stood in need of pardon or forgiveness. There was no vindictive justice, for there was no object capable of punishment.

But you will object that I seem to reject God's vindictive justice and deny his anger against sin and sinners. I answer: not at all, for I only say that none of these are to be found in the solitary and primary being of the Deity, and are only attributed to him inasmuch as he has introduced himself into the properties of eternal nature.

As the opening of the eye reveals itself and the heart, so it also manifests the Holy Ghost as the outgoing emanation of both eye and heart, a sweet, pleasant, outflowing life or power like a breath or gust of air, conveyed through the heart of the Son as the golden oil transmitted through the golden pipe of the Son's essential love. This is the active life and power of the Holy Trinity, which finishes the work of true regeneration in apostatized creatures.

Finally, when the eye of eternity opens, it manifests God's divine body.

But you object: God has no body, but is a pure spirit. To this I answer: God has no organic body like men, nor like those of the glorified saints and angels. But God has a body such as becomes his high, spiritual, refined nature. For the immense deep of the abyssal globe of eternity is God's universal, incomprehensible omnipresent body. This is the eternal corporeity of the Holy Trinity, which comprehends all things, being comprehended of none but itself; it is universally in all beings, and diffused through all beings; nothing can keep it out or shut it up. It is a free liberty in itself; it stands free from all essences, only so far as it pleases itself to unite with any essence. With regard to this universal body, it is the Alpha and Omega; all things proceed from it, so it is the first, and all things subsist in it, so it is the last. Thus we see that the Holy Trinity have the globe of eternity for their body in which they act and move. This body is Wisdom's crystalline glass, wherein all things are truly and intellectually represented to the eye of the mind; it is in this deep abyss of the globe of eternity that all those divine mysteries are discovered and manifested. For in this mirror of Wisdom all the depths of the Deity stand openly represented to the eye of the spirit.

Those images and figures which the opening of the eye manifests are not shadows and empty representations, but real and substantial ones; they are not only figures of heavenly things but the heavenly things themselves. These figures are unchangeable, because they are essential to the Holy Trinity. The eye is essential to the Father; the flaming heart of love is essential to the Son; and the outflowing breath of power is essential to the Holy Ghost. Though in eternal nature, in the darkness, the eye of the Father appears dark, wrathful, and terrible, yet in the light it is pleasant and full of love. Yet the eye is not changed by these variations, though diversified by the light and darkness.

Concerning Wisdom and the Most Holy Place

The following names are given to this third court by the spirit of God: still eternity, unutterable rest, silence, and stillness, the presence chamber of the spirit of eternity, the king of kings, the rock of wonders.

The essential difference of this place is the majestic silence and awful stillness with which it is continually filled. This is such a stillness as surpasses not only all expressions, but also all thoughts and imaginations. Here all the glory and magnificence of monarchs is but a shadow or nothing.

The first wonder in this place, the rock of wonders, is the spirit of eternity, which fills the total deep abyss with itself, with all power. Here the glory of the power of the Deity is seen nakedly, openly and without a veil, eye to eye, and face to face, the sight of which causes ravishing ecstasies, unexpressible joys, and transporting admiration to fill the heart of the beholder, it being a sight so glorious as no words can express, nor thoughts represent to the mind, as being beyond all comprehension.

The second wonder in this place is the Holy Trinity, and the third is God's Wisdom, who springs from God's eternal eye. By this Wisdom, all the desire and motions of the Deity are ordered. God's Wisdom is a bright ray or glance issuing from the eye of eternity; therefore she is termed the brightness or clarity of the Godhead, and a pure breath from the majesty of the almighty. Wisdom is co-essential with the Holy Trinity. She is clearly distinguishable from the eye, and the spirit of the eye, for she is only a brightness, glance, or ray proceeeding from it, and is consequently subordinate to the Blessed Trinity.

The essential property of the divine Wisdom is her virgin purity, for she is free from all desire, will, and motion of her own. She moves not, but as she is moved, and acts not, but as she is acted on by the spirit of eternity. She is an eternal stillness in herself. She is a thousand times brighter and purer than the sun, fairer than the moon. She is exalted above all things because of her beauty and immaculate purity; she is purity and virginity in the abstract. She cannot be touched by sin, evil, or self, because she cannot mix with nor incline to anything except the esssential love of God. She is free from all essences whatever, being nothing else but the unspotted mirror of the glory and excellency of God.

Wisdom is a revealer of the mysteries and hidden wonders of the Deity. She is the golden key of the eternal eye by which all the wonders of the Trinity are unlocked. As the office of the Holy Ghost is to create all things, the office of Wisdom is to manifest and reveal all things. She brings forth nothing, but only discovers and manifests whatever the Holy Trinity are

pleased to bring forth. Wisdom is the companion of the eternal eye; she is like a handmaid waiting upon the Holy Trinity to publish and make known their counsels, secrets, and wonders.
Wisdom gives light to the deep abyss of the still eternity.

But you will object that the Scriptures and divine philosophers have spoken concerning wisdom in another manner than I have done. To this I answer that they speak of Wisdom after the production of eternal nature, as Wisdom is introduced into the seven forms of eternal nature; but I speak of Wisdom's existence with the Holy Trinity in the still eternity before eternal nature was brought forth.

The Seven Spirits and the Simplified Spirits of God

We now turn to the seven spirits of God, which stand before the throne of the Holy Trinity. St. John often mentions these in the book of Revelation, but he speaks of them as they were seen by him on Mount Zion in the New Jerusalem after their being introduced into the working properties of pure nature, whereas I treat of them as they were seen in the still eternity, before the existence of pure nature out of which the New Jerusalem was created. Accordingly, we are to distinguish between these seven spirits and the seven generating fountain-spirits out of which pure nature and her elements were generated, according to the highly enlightened Böhme.

These seven spirits of God are the various outgoing powers immediately proceeding from the body of the Holy Ghost; they are the true fruits of the spirit. For as the supreme Unity becomes a Trinity, so the Trinity varies itself into a Septenary, or seven spirits. These seven spirits are co-essential and co-eternal with the Trinity, but not co-equal with them. The seven spirits are the high princely counsellors of the divine majesty; all the secrets of the Holy Trinity are revealed to them, for the Holy Trinity does nothing without them, in that they perform and execute the will of the Deity.

These spirits are not personal spirits, as the angels are, who appear in organic bodies; they are pure simplified spirits without composition; they resemble the supreme unity and simplicity of the Deity, from which they proceed.
You must not think that the Deity is solitary or unattended except by these seven spirits, for there are innumerable pure simplified spirits that stand ready in humble resigned obedience to execute the will and perform the pleasure of the Father of spirits. Pure and simple spirits exist without eternal nature in the still eternity; mixed spirits are those created out of eternal nature and exist the same as all angelic spirits do. They are said to be mixed because they do not immediately proceed from the supreme Unity, as

simple spirits do, but are created out of nature's forms. Those who suppose the angels are spirits of the first degree of perfection are mistaken: they are indeed the most perfect created out of the principle of eternal nature, but they do not reach the perfection of those simple spirits who proceed from the Unity in the still eternity. They are most simple essences and powers, free from all admixture or duality, without any angelical or other figure, and are eternal unities, proceeding from the supreme Unity itself.

I here subjoin a figure wherein, by way of likeness, you may conceive in what manner these simplified spirits, the inhabitants of the still eternity, were represented to the eye of my spirit:

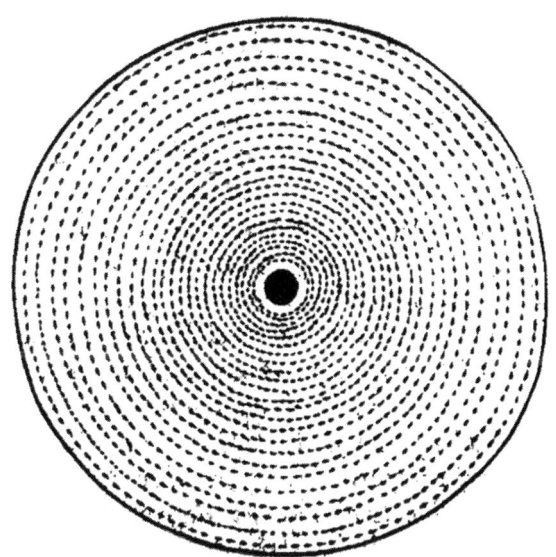

This figure represents the still eternity; the black spot in the center of this circle represents the central eye of eternity, and the black points, with which the whole circumference is filled denote those pure simplified spirits that are the inhabitants of the still eternity.

The simplified spirits are numberless and distinct from one another, like stars in the firmament.

They are all alike and co-equal; they are all of the same essence, and all equally eternal, and appear like bright sparks or eyes. They all resemble the central eye of the Deity. They are lights from light, and nothing other than the eye of eternity multiplying itself through the immeasurable extent of the still eternity.

The simplified spirits are generated by God out of himself, in the likeness of himself, and for himself. How were they generated by God? This I confess is a great mystery, but we can say that these simplified spirits did from all eternity exist ideally in the eye of eternity,, and these ideas were actually manifested before all worlds, for they are ideas conceived in the divine mind, which then desired that they come into being. The Holy Ghost then brought them forth.

All pure simplified spirits were brought forth out of divine love's eternal essentiality, out of the eternal flaming heart of God's love. This love gives unity and harmony to all things. There is no unity in heaven nor on earth but what derives from love.

Love is a perfect and absolute liberty. Nothing can move love but love, nothing touch love, but love, nor anything constrain love, but love. It is free from all things, gives laws to itself, and those laws are the laws of liberty. Love is all strength and power. Make a diligent search through heaven and earth, and you'll find nothing so powerful as love. What is stronger than hell and death? Love is the triumphant conquerer of both. The great effect of love is to turn all things into its own nature, which is goodness, sweetness, and perfection. This is that divine power that turns water into wine, sorry and anguish into exulting and triumphing joys. It changes evil into good, and all imperfection into perfection. It restores what is fallen and degenerated into its primary beauty, excellence, and perfection. It is the divine stone, the white stone with a Name written on it that no one knows save he who has it. In a word, it is the divine nature, it is God himself, whose essential property it is to assimilate all things with himself, to reconcile all things to himself, be they in heaven or on earth, by means of this divine elixir, whose transforming power nothing can withstand. Love makes all things fruitful.

These simplified spirits, then, are first in the eye of the Father, as so many ideas, which ideas afterwards are fruitful seeds in the womb of love, and are brought to manifestation by the all-effecting power of the Holy Ghost, assisted by Wisdom. Wherefore it does not appear impossible that the unity of love's essence should multiply and vary itself into innumerable offspring. How many sparks proceed from one fire? How much more, then, is the Heart of God able to multiply itself?

These simplified spirits were brought forth for the manifestation of the Deity, for had the divine nature continued shut up in itself in the still eternity, without bringing forth itself, it would never have been known to any but itself. And so for the manifestation of the Triune Deity were these simplified spirits brought forth to be inhabitants of the still eternity. They were brought forth for the manifestation of the virtues and excellencies of the divine essence in the still eternity—that is, his eternity, infinity, unity, simplicity, liberty, goodness, perfection, and happiness. Thus one of the ends of the production of these spirits was that the mystery of the divine being might be known to others besides itself in the still eternity. Therefore were these spirits produced, who are all eye, and every way able to dwell upon the blissful contemplation of the Triune Deity.

The simplified spirits have no souls, or any personal organic corporeity, but they do have a body which is common to them all: the temple body of the Holy Ghost, which fills the whole circumference of that most holy place in which they do all dwell.

These inhabitants are intellectual spirits, endowed with understanding and will, and with the spiritual senses of seeing, hearing, smelling, tasting, and feeling, whereby they are enabled to discern the object of the still eternity. They behold the Trinity face to face, hearken to his still and awful voice, are refreshed by perceiving the odors that continually perfume the most holy place, taste and feed upon the outflowing sweetness of the Deity, and feel nothing but the eternal goodness of him who with his fullness fills the still eternity.

Their minds are continually taken up and delighted with the beatific vision of the Deity; their wills are satisfied in the enjoyment of the chiefest good; their senses are pleased with the most ravishing objects; and they continually bathe themselves in the rivers of unknown delights that proceed from the heart of the Deity without intermission.

Their speaking to one another is thought; whatever they but think is answered immediately; their thoughts are all known to one another and forthwith answered. They all see through one eye, hear through one ear, all live in one heart, and from one center of life, breathe from one breath, will from one spirit, and stand in one body.

On Eternal Nature

The orb of eternal nature is the original ground of all worlds, both visible and invisible, of heaven and angels, of hell and devils, of all spirits good or bad, and indeed, all created essences. Hence spring light and darkness, good and evil, life and death, joy and sorrow, wrath and love, happiness and misery, and unity and contrariety. It is a grand mystery not made known to former ages; for in this consists all secrets and mysteries belonging to our salvation.

By coming to know the mysteries of this eternal nature, we shall come to know and comprehend the deep mysteries of God, who has brought himself forth into eternal nature as a ground where he might be manifested to his intellectual creatures. This eternal nature is the true ground of all created beings and so of all true knowledge. By the right understanding of this mystery, we shall come to understand the secret meaning of many mystical Scriptures. This is a library and academy in itself, and can teach the original ground of all arts and sciences. It is worth our labor to consider this little book, which will teach the way of true wisdom and knowledge. This has been revealed to that enlightened philosopher Jacob Böhme, who could be understood by few, but I have here endeavored to lay open to your view all the seven working forms of eternal nature and the ground of all things, without any convering, and in as plain words as I could invent, so that even one of the meanest capacity who is willing to learn and throw aside pride, envy, and high-mindedness, may be taught and benefited. For the time of the lily is at hand.

Speak not against that which you don't understand, and judge not others lest you be judged. I have many years studied this little book. Be wary of vain philosophers and academic knowledge that have devoured the spirit of God and served only to make men highminded and proud, despiring their brothers, crying out that all is fancy and delusion that does not agree with them. I am not against humane learning; I have known what it is, but I would not have it set above the spirit of God. For God has said he will destroy the wisdom of the wise, and make himself known to babes.

The wisdom of this world is indeed by folly at best. I confess myself the least of all saints, and not worthy of the knowledge of these deep mysteries that God has revealed to me and manifested to my eternal spirit, but God has thought it good to use me as an instrument in his hand, the effect of which I leave to God, desiring to be serviceable to you.

Yours in the love of Jesus,
JP M.D.

The Abyssal Nothing and Eternal Nature

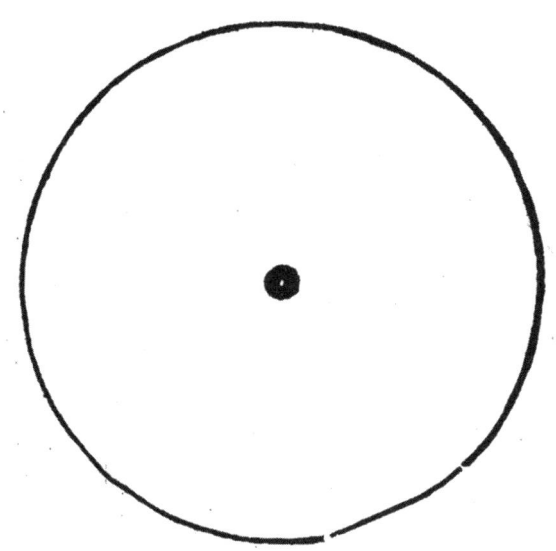

This circle represents the principle of eternal nature. The black spot in the midst of the circle represents God's eternal eye. The wide space within the circle is the chaos or the abyssal nothing, the ground of all essences, and yet no essence to be seen in it. Because I will make mention of the word *principle*, I think it proper to define it here. By the word *principle*, I do not mean the first constitutive beginnings of things, from whence they take their being, in the same sense in which the four elements by some, and salt, sulphur, and mercury by others, are called the principles of all things. By a *principle*, I mean an original source and fountain-essence, formed by an agent into a spherical circumference. Not every essence makes a principle, but only one, the fruitful mother of all the essences contained in its own circumference and kingdom. A principle is passive, considered without the active spirit in the center that moves it.

Eternal nature is a principle created by God out of the abyssal chaos, containing the seven operative powers for the production of all things.

What is eternal nature? It was a pure essence, free from sin and evil and all mixture of imperfection; she was then all fair, clear, spotless, faultless, and sinless. The cause of eternal nature is the Triune Deity in joint cooperation. God can subsist without nature, but eternal nature's essence cannot subsist without the Triune Deity. God comprehends eternal nature, but eternal nature ccannot comprehend him.

The great mystery lies here, in knowing how eternal nature proceeds from God's essence. Eternal nature proceeds from God's abyssal essence, generated out of himself. This abyssal essence is an immense, deep, empty space, a bottomless and boundless abyss. Yet I do not say it is without beginning, for God generated this abyssal essence out of his own eternal essence, as was manifested to my sight by God's spirit. I could not write of it as I do, had I not seen the pattern in the mount of eternity. God's eternal will formed this abyss into a circle or globe, for the desiring will looking into itself and finding nothing but himself, put an end to himself, and so formed a round or globe.

The abyssal essence is a deep, immense, boundless, empty space, and is therefore called a ground without ground. When I say boundless, I do not mean its bounds are uncomprehended by God, but in relation to our spirits. In this empty, immense space there is nothing to be seen, no darkness, no fire, no light, no creature. It is an unsearchable deep without any essence, thought it is the ground of all essence, and that from whence eternal nature's essence proceeds.

The abyssal essence is called by mystical writers the divine chaos, and the original essence of all essences, from whence all created essences, principles, and centers proceed. Böhme writes thus: if the spirit of the soul could come into the eternal nothing, he would come into that original gound whence eternal nature and all creatures did proceed. He further writes that if the spirit of the soul could sink down into this eternal nothing and abyssal still essence, then he would come into that ground where God was when he brought forth eternal nature and creatures. Thus I have led you to the original ground of eternal nature, the abyssal still essence of eternity.

This abyssal essence is generated out of God's essence, that is, out of himself, by himself, and for the pleasure of himself, and is himself. But if you will ask further what this essence is that is thus generated out of himself, I can give no other answer, for futher than this none but the Triune Deity can tell.

What is above this abyssal essence? I answer: the all-seeing eye, the eternal free will of the Deity in the still eternity. The original globe of eternity is above it and distinct from it: this divine chaos is a middle gulf between the eternal world—where stands the still eternity in its eternal unity, simplicity, and pure Deity—and eternal nature's essence and working powers. You are likewise to distinguish the globe of eternity from the light world, in which paradise, the angelical world, the glassy sea, Mount Zion, and the New Jerusalem are placed. Though these by called by us the heavenly world, as in truth they are, yet they differ from the still eternity. All these worlds, paradise, the angelical world, and others, spring forth out of the light eternity, and the light eternity is born out of eternal nature's essence.

Still eternity in the eternal world stands before, above, and without eternal nature's essences.

Eternal nature is God's workhouse, wherein he has whatever is materially required for creation. In the eternal nothing is no actual essence, but in eternal nature, all essences for creation are actually brought forth by God's wisdom and power.

What is the original matter of eternal nature? I answer: Fire and light with their essential properties, and the four eternal elements of fire, water, air and earth, for if these were taken away, eternal nature would cease to be.

Fire is the first matter and ground of eternal nature's essence. Here a multitude of words will but darken the manner of its birth. The highly illuminated Böhme has written how this eternal element was brought into existence by the will of God, but there are few that can understand him, and those that do comprehend a great mystery. Reason with all its academic knowledge cannot comprehend it, it being only discerned by intellectual sight. Though in the glass of divine wisdom I have seen out this element out of eternal nothing was brought into an eternal something, essential fire, yet I do not find it necessary to explain it any further at this time.

The word *eternal* here is to be understood *a parte post*, and not *a parte ante*, as the Scholastics have it, for nothing is eternal but the Triune Deity.

What is the nature of eternal fire? This eternal element is created by God to be a mighty, penetrating, consuming essence. The first of its properties is darkness, which consists in astringent harshness, from which arises bitterness with its prickliness, and out of this bitter prickliness arises the eternal woe and tormenting anguish, called the sting of the bitter anguish. From this arises the fire-essence. To it belongs fierceness, fieriness, wrathfulness, sternness, consuming, devouring, flying up and elevating itself. Without these, it would be weak and feeble.

Wherein is the goodness of this fire-essence? Its essential properties are all good in relation to the end for which they were conceived. There is no evil property to be found in this fire-essence. Since it was created by God, it must needs be good, for no evil can proceed from God.

Water is the second matter of eternal nature's essence. Water is a meek, mild, soft, gentle essence, for as the fire-essence is the ground of fierceness, water is the ground of meekness. This meek essence, with its qualities of softness, mildness, gentleness, refreshingness, sincking down, heaviness, is the ground of eternal light; it is the womb of the meek light, whence springs pleasantness, delightfulness, joyfulness, and gladness. Its production is to allay the fierceness of the fire-essence and to be its antagonist. To the fierce, fiery, harsh darkness, the water opposes its sweetness and pleasantness; to the anguish, wrath, and devouring property of the fire, it opposes the joyfulness of its love-fire essence, and to the mounting elevation of the fire, it opposes its sinking-down. Here you see that the beauty, excellence, and strength of the water consists in its meekness, mildness, softness, gentleness, and sweetness.

The third element is eternal air, a brisk, cooling, refeshing, reviving, quickening, pleasant essence, breath, or wind. It blows up the fire, lest it be suffocated, and gives motion to the water, driving away the dark clouds from the light-essence. It is the food of all the properties, and also the chariot of the spirit of God, who rides upon the wings of this wind to separate the precious and the vile, the wheat and the chaff. Its essential properties are clarity, transparency, volatility, levity, celerity, and penetrability.

The fourth element is eternal earth, whose properties are ponderosity, corporeity, and transparency. It is not like the outward elementary earth, gross and opaque, but rather is a transparent crystalline earth, yet gives essentiality and corporeity to the other three elements.

Wisdom's art appears in reducing them to harmony and in their moving in and through one another. The harsh darkness is serviceable to the meek light, for darkness is the subject through which light displays itself; were there no darkness, there would be no light. The fierceness of the fire gives strength to the meek water-essence, and the meekness of the water allys the fierceness of the fire; air keeps the fire from being suffocated, and the earth gives them all a body to act and move in.

Thus I define eternal nature as subsisting in a sixfold working property, inseparable one from the other. Darkness generates harshness, harshness or bitterness anguish, anguish fire, fire water, water light or love-fire, and love-fire air; thus they generate one another, but in the seventh they all rest as in one only ground. Eternal nature subsists in six working properties in one only ground or substance. They all have one beginning, one mother, and in their union they constitute the wrestling wheel of eternal nature, wherein sometimes one is uppermost, sometimes another, sometimes darkness, sometimes light, sometimes anguish, sometimes joy. Yet though they be undivided, for distinction's sake, we may place darkness in the first place, as the root of the dark fire-essence, which is the center of eternal nature. The prickly stinging bitterness or harshness is in the second place, anguish in the third, fire in the fourth, water, light, and love-fire in the fifth, air in the sixth, and last is earth.

Perhaps someone will object that I contradict Böhme, who places darkness and light opposite to one another and makes the fire a distinct center from the light. To this I answer that what Böhme writes is most true, but he is writing of eternal nature in its fallen or degenerate state, whereas I am speaking of it in its original spotless purity. Böhme speaks of God in nature, but I speak of eternal nature's birth in God's introducing himself into nature's essence. So I do not in the least contradict Böhme's writings.

Eternal nature was produced for manifestation, that the Triune Deity might manifest themselves, and together with themselves the still eternity, that they might no longer be hid in their abstracted nature of pure spirit and naked Deity. Eternal nature was created so that the glorious attributes of God might be displayed and made known; it is the subject matter out of which all creations and worlds might be brought forth.

What awakened the first thought in the spirit of eternity to create eternal nature? None can tell this but the spirit of eternity itself. But we may learn that the spirit of the Holy Trinity is magical. Thus God brought forth the eternal world, the still eternity, with all its wonders, out of Himself, by Himself, and for Himself to dwell in magically, and after the same manner the divine chaos and eternal nature were brought forth. The spirit of the Holy Trinity wills and acts from nothing other than its pure magia, for it is a wise, intelligent spirit, grounded in the divine magia.

There is no use of reason in the still eternity, for the divine magia supplies its room; neither is reason made use of in paradise, nor in the angelical world, nor in the New Jerusalem, because reason belongs only to the spirit of this outward world. And however enlightened reason may be exalted by some, yet my spirit knows it to be an eternal infallible truth that there is no use of reason but in this Babylonish principle, and the kingdom of the beast.

Eternal nature was brought forth that it might be a garment of the Holy Trinity, a vesture to clothe their pure naked Deity, for as the soul is hid and wrapped up in the body, and the body in its clothes, so the Holy Trinity is wrapped up in eternal nature's essence, and in the creatures thence proceeding. Blessed are they who through all these wiles and disguisements can find him who is the desire of all nations, they who in this rubbish can find the pearl of great price, which if we search deep enough we cannot fail of, for the Holy Trinity in their pure Deity is the innermost kernel of all things, hid under eternal nature's essence and all her working forms or elements.

Eternal nature was produced to be a medium between two extremes, God and the creature, whereby God might communicate himself to creatures, and creatures might have fellowship with him.

The still divine essence, by entering into the contrariety of eternal nature, manifests the glory of the majesty, and triumphing, exulting joy, which were not to be found in the still eternity before the working properties of eternal nature were brought forth.

Eternal nature was brought forth to be the true *primum mobile*, the source of all motion and action. In still eternity there is nothing but stillness, quiet, and rest, and that which passes all thought and conception of man. That spirit only knows it who has been taken up into it.

Eternal nature was produced so that the single essence of the Holy Trinity might be manifested in distinction according to the properties of eternal nature. Thus the Father is manifest in Fire, the Son in Water, and the Holy Ghost in Air.

Finally, eternal nature was produced so that all the ideas, forms, and patterns in the divine mind might become actual and substantial, which could not be brought to pass in the still eternity, nor without the working properties of eternal nature.

What kind of principle is eternal nature? Eternal nature is an eternal essence, for whatever is immediately created by God out of the divine chaos is eternal because it proceeds from an eternal root. Eternal nature is an original essence, the first created essence out of whose fruitful womb all created essences proceed. It is the first essence of all essences, and the ground and source of them. There is nothing above, before, or beyond it, except the Holy Trinity in the still eternity. All essences proceed from it, whether temporal or eternal, for time itself is rooted in eternity.

But how can eternal nature be the first original essence, since the eternal world and the divine chaos are before it? The answer is obvious: I do not say that eternal nature is the first essence, but the first created essence. The eternal world and divine chaos were not created by God, but generated out of him.

Yet isn't God the essence of all essences, and the first matter of all things? I answer: God is the original essence of all essences, as he is the creator of eternal nature's essence out of the divine chaos. Yet God is the essence of all essences remotely but not immediately, for all created essences do immediately proceed from eternal nature and not from God, for the divine chaos and eternal nature stand between them and God. If all creatures had immediately proceeded from God, they must all have been a perfect unity, without any duality, diversity, or contrariety, because God's essence from which they proceeded was such. But we find that all created essences are not a perfect unity; diversity and duality is found in them, which is not found in the divine essence. Therefore we must conclude that they did not immediately proceed from God's essence.

Eternal nature is a middle essence, placed by God between the eternal world and the angelical, and this visible creation, and is the original ground from whence all middle worlds proceed. Were not eternal nature a middle essence, there would be no middle worlds, no middle states, nothing but the still eternity. Scripture [Hebrews I.2] tells us of worlds in the plural number, which must be these middle worlds of which I here have spoken.

Eternal nature is in itself an invisible essence, for it is the ground from whence all invisible worlds proceed. Even this outward visible world was made of an invisible matter. The things which are seen were not made of the things that do appear [Hebrews 11.3].

Eternal nature and all its forms are good, not the chiefest good, which is only to be found in the divine essence, but endowed by God with a natural goodness, free from evil.

Evil is not in God, nor in eternal nature.

But what is the source of evil? I answer: the mutability of the creature is the cause of evil. For though all things be created good by God, yet they are not immutably so, but may become evil. We will speak no more of this matter here, because this is not the proper place to do so, since we are here only treating eternal nature as it came out of God's hand, and before any creatures were brought forth out of it.

You may object that Jacob Böhme makes eternal nature the ground of good and evil. But I answer that what Böhme writes of eternal nature is very true, for he does not make eternal nature in its original purity the ground of evil. Böhme is not well understood because sometimes he speaks of eternal nature in its original purity, and shortly after speaks of it with reference to its fallen state. This, being not sufficiently noted by unwary readers, makes them conclude that Böhme makes eternal nature in its original purity the ground of evil, which is contrary to the whole scope of his writings. Böhme was sensible of this mistake, and so wrote that there was a veil upon his writings that would hinder all those who were not born again from having a right understanding of them. Böhme, when he attributes evil to eternal nature, considers it in its fallen state as it became infected with the second or hellish principle by the fall of Lucifer, and I do fully agree with him, but I am speaking of eternal nature in its pure undefiled state.

If there were no darkness, there would be no light, and hence darkness is no evil essence. Nor is the bitterness and sting of the anguish evil in itself, because they are the cause of the triumphing joy. Nor the fire, though it be a fierce devouring essence, can be considered evil, for when these qualities are penetrated by water, they become the cause of pleasure and triumphing joy. Fire as it was originally in eternal nature is no evil essence. Nor can it be said that the contrariety found in the forms and properties of eternal nature makes them evil, for all six forms of nature are united and harmonized in the seventh, where no strife, contrariety or opposition is to be found, nor anything that might be denominated evil. In this harmony of the essential forms of eternal nature does the intrinsic goodness of eternal nature consist.

Let us consider again the forms of eternal nature. We begin with the darkness, and the sting of anguish. Out of darkness comes the fire, and the fire needs the darkness in which to exist. The fire comes out of the abyssal chaos by the eternal speaking word of power. The nature of the fire-spirit is an eternal hunger and a dry painful thirst in itself. The more it hungers, the more it is attracted to its own fuel, sulphur, mercury, and sal-nitre, but it cannot satisfy itself. The water-essence is the food of the fire that allays its hunger, and so fire finds its eternal refreshment in it. Yet the fire-spirit cannot reach water by rising, only by sinking down deep in its own root. When it quenches its dry insatiable thirst in water, it is transported with joy, and says O blessed element! How can you be so near me, even in my own root and center, and I am not aware of you? I have tasted your sweetness and am refreshed. Mingle your meekness with my strength and fierceness, that my anguishing hunger and thirst may no longer be felt by me.

Then arises the light, which makes the water clear and transparent, the fire bright and luminous, and hid the darkness in its own glory. O the wonderful pleasant birth of light! By penetrating the essences of eternal nature, light makes them wholly meek, swee, soft, and delightful, so that nothing but a pleasing sight, sweet smell, delightful taste, ravishing sound, and soft pleasant feelings is to be found.

The air-spirit moderates the wrath-fire, but also blows up the love-fire essence, which is the loveliest, pleasantest, and sweetest birth of them all, as Jacob Böhme says. As soon as this child of love is born, the whole birth of eternal nature stands in great triumph of divine joy; all its powers and essences become substantial, and they do see, hear, smell, taste, and feel one another in the most ravishing joyfulness beyond words and this pen's expression. For the love-fire gives itself for food to all the properties of nature; it becomes eternal bread and wine, wherewith they are fed and refreshed forever. They cry out: O love! you have satisfied our hunger and quenched our thirst, you have filled us with the highest exulting joys. Behold, we desire no longer to have any will of our own, but that all our wills may be thine.

When this love-essence mingles with the spirit, it begets in it a divine and spiritual understanding, and opens his spiritual senses of seeing, hearing, tasting, smelling, and feeling. Thus the blind properties of nature come to see spiritually and intellectually, the deaf to hear, the dumb to sing, the barren to become fruitful. When this love-fire-tincture enters into the dark-fire-forms and penetrates the burning sulphur, poisonous mercury, and salt-nitre of the fire-spirit and change them into its own nature, there arises such triumphing joy, ravishing extasy and exultation as none can imagine but those that have felt them. This love-fire tincture proceeds from the union of the fire and the light, and is the joy and end of eternal nature; nor is there any birth to be looked for or enjoyed beyond this birth of love.

And in the last place, the creator brings forth the seventh form, in which all the six working properties act, the dwelling place of the eternal earth. Here they dwell in triumphant joy. Thus you see the birth of eternal nature, complete and perfect.

The Holy Trinity created eternal nature to be a palace to dwell in. Now as in a royal palace we must pass through many rooms before we come to the presence-chamber of the prince, so in eternal nature the forms of darkness must be passed trhough and after these the fire and water, before we can come to the love-fire, which the Holy Trinity has chosen for his presence chamber. God will not have his creatures rush in all of a sudden into his all-glorious presence, and therefore has ordered it that many doors must be passed by them, and many locks opened, before they can come to his presence, whom to see and know is eternal bliss and happiness.

Thrice happy is the man who by walking this path of pure nature has passed the gates of darkness, bitterness, and anguish, and after them the gate of the fierce-fire, and at length through water, light, and air has made his way to the love-fire essence, where he meets with eternal rest, liberty, and triumphant joy.

Here the end has found the beginning, and the beginning and the end are joined together, never to be parted again forever.

Eternal nature's principle is to be the conduit-pipe through which the golden oil and water of life, together with the divine virtue of the heavenly tincture, is conveyed to the creature. Pure nature's principle is the silver-pipe through which the golden oil of the holy tincture that flows from the union of fire and light is conveyed; it is the means by which the Holy Trinity, with the wonders of eternity, come to be manifested, felt, tasted, and enjoyed.

Eternal nature's principle is the field in which is hid the inestimable Pearl of the Holy Trinity; it is the cabinet wherein is contained the jewel of wonder, the Deity in pure humanity.

Whoever finds this pearl does, together with it, find all the wonders of the Holy Trinity. The pearl is indeed one thing and the field or rich cabinet another, yet both field and cabinet are very useful to keep and conceal the precious stone of eternal wisdom that is fast locked up in this cabinet, and lies deep buried in this field. Whowever will find it must dig deep for it.

But you will say: where shall I find this field? I answer: *the field is yourself*. If you can find in yourself the union of fire and light, and these two qualifying together in one essence, then you have met with the place where this noble stone is hid, and you need seek no further.

Soli Sapienti Deo Gloria.

On God in Eternal Nature

The mystical divines mention two great mysteries in the divine nature. The first is the Trinity in Unity and Unity in Trinity, which concerns the Deity in their single, solitary, and abstracted essence. The second mystery is the Deity in Humanity and Humanity in the Deity, which concerns God introduced and subsisting in eternal nature. I have in the first part of this discourse treated the first of these, and now intend to speak of the latter, that is, of how God has introduced himself into the principle of nature.

In the first place, when I say that God has introduced himself into eternal nature, I understand that the blessed Trinity, Father, Son, and Holy Ghost, have introduced themselves into eternal nature, the Father with his intellectual all-seeing eye, the Son with his flaming heart of love, and the Holy Ghost with his outflowing acting power. In the second place, when I say that God introduced himself into eternal nature, I include the eternal Wisdom that God introduced together with himself.
In the third place, God introduced hiimself into eternal nature together with his essential love, the holy nature of the Trinity.

Some may object that the divine nature consists not only in love, but also in light and life. But I answer that love, in the sense I take it, includes light and life, for this essential love is all light and life, so that neither death nor darkness can come near it. We must not think that the divine nature is changed by being brought into and clothed with eternal nature, and love turned to wrath, or meekness to severity. No, by no means: for as God is all love in himself, so he is the same in eternal nature.

But you will say: how can this be reconciled with Scripture, which attributes wrath, anger, severity and justice to God? I answer that when the Scripture speaks of God's anger, wrather, and severity, it refers to God's manifesting himself in and through eternal nature as it is infected and defiled by sin. Whereas when I say that the manifestation of God in nature is all love, I speak of nature in its purity, before it was infected by the fall of Lucifer, and when all its forms and properties were harmonized to the most perfect concord and unity.

God introduced the seven spirits before the throne together with himself into eternal nature; else these seven spirits could never have been manifested in eternal nature's principle, but Scripture often makes mention of them as introduced into eternal nature. They were represented to John in the first chapter of Revelation as existing in Mount Zion, or the New Jerusalem principle that was brought forth out of eternal nature.

When we say that the Holy Trinity have introduced themselves into eternal nature, we mean nothing but the union of the blessed Trinity with eternal nature, and eternal nature's union with the blessed Trinity, which is the full meaning of God's introduction of himself into eternal nature's principle. Here the Deity subsists in its eternal humanity, and eternal humanity subsists in union with the Deity: God in nature, and nature in God; and thus God and nature are in one another.

The union of God with eternal nature is a true, real, essential, and most intimate union. In every union these three things are to be found: the uniter, the thing united, and the union itself, which joins uniter and united together. The united is the blessed Trinity, the thing united is the principle of eternal nature, and the union of them both is the divine nature of love. It is a kind of incorporation, the uniter and united penetrating and mixing with one another. Therefore this union of God and eternal nature in love's essence is compared to a nuptial union, because God has as it were espoused himself with eternal nature as a pure, spotless, and undefiled virgin, in an indissoluble bond, which is essential love.

But you will ask: can God's love be turned into anger? I answer by denying that love can be changed into anger in eternal nature, as she stands in purity and perfection, before the coming in of sin, because in that state neither eternal nature nor anything in it could be the subject of God's anger, hatred, severity, or justice.

In fallen nature we perceive the effects of God's love and hatred, mercy and justice, sweetness and severity, yet in pure nature, nothing can ever be found but the effects of an unchangeable bond.

The Trinity brought themselves into pure nature's principle for the manifestation of themselves in and by it. For though they were manifested to themselves and simplified spirits in the still eternity, yet they desired a further manifestation of themselves to creatures that lay hid in the womb of eternal nature, and for this reason they entered into union with it.

In the still eternity there were indeed an infinite number of simplified spirits, who dwelling in the center of love, did glorify and exalt the divine nature of love. But the design of God was to have his eternal love glorified and exalted in an infinite variety of creatures and beings, and so make up the divine consort and harmony.

The eternal goodwill and purpose of the Holy Trinity was to manifest their own glory in the creation of worlds, and an infinite variety of creatures, out of eternal nature's principle.

God introduced himself into eternal nature for the glorification of nature by means of its union with the divine essence of love. It was for the glorification of nature, that nature might be exalted to the highest degree of glory it was capable of by its union with the Deity.

Appendix:

The Archetypal Globe

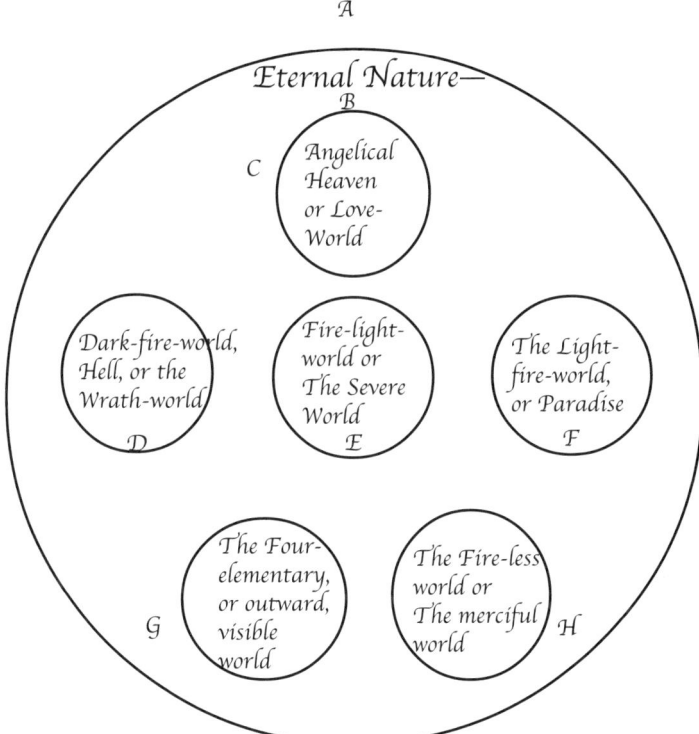

Through faith we understand that the worlds were framed

An explanation of the eight worlds and their centers

The letter A affords a view of the Archetypal globe or world, the first, which encompasses the others.
B is eternal nature, which encloses all the worlds.
C is the angelical world.
D is the dark fire-world.
E is the fire-light world.
F is the light-fire world.
G is the four-elementary world.
H is the light-fireless world.

We may further observe that all worlds or principles are comprehended in the first, the eternal world, which is contained by none. Another thing to be observed is that eternal nature is the second world, and contains six worlds in itself, situated in the order of their production (according to the letters above). Finally, we are to take notice of the penetration of the worlds one through another, without admixture. Thus the eternal world passes through all those which it comprehends within its circumference, just as God fills this world and dwells in it. For as God penetrates through all, so does this world, which could well be called in this sense the body of God. Likewise does eternal nature penetrate the six worlds, and are contained in its circumference. Each of the six worlds penetrate through one another, yet without admixture, because each has a distinct center and principle. This much shall suffice in explanation of this diagram.

Index

Abyssal Globe, 9, 12, 32 ff.
Angels, 4
Apocatastasis, 17
Ashmole, Elias, 2
Bathurst, Anne, 2
Böhme, Jacob, 6, 35, 56, 61, 66, 73
Brice, Edmund, 2, 3
Bromley, Thomas, 2, 3, 21
Buddhism, 22
Catachresis, 8-9, 20
Chardin, Teilhard de, 19
Corbin, Henry, 23
Eliade, Mircea, 24
Elijah, 17
Eternal Nature, 7, 15-16, 28, 55-57, 58-75, 77-80
Eternal World, 32 ff.
Eye, 32 ff., 44
Great Plague, 5
Heart of God, 42-43
History, 19-20
Holy Spirit, 8, 29, 37, 77
Holy Trinity, 11, 28, 29-31, 38, 74
Hooker, Edward, 8
Matthew, 17
Nothing, 58
Novalis, 18
Leade, Jane, 10
Light world, 3
Non-sectarianism, 27
Oxenbridge, Joanna, 2
Pearl, 76, 81
Pordage, John, *passim*

Regeneration, 8
Simplified Spirits, 14, 49-55
Spiritus mundi, 19-20
Sophia, 6, 11
Sufism, 22
Transfiguration, 17
Ungrund, 22
Via negativa, 22
Wisdom, 47-49